P9-DDV-826

EAGLES
Must Soar

EAGLES
Must Soar

7 SIMPLE STRATEGIES
FOR LIVING A LIFE
WITH CERTAINTY

Barry Siskind

John Wiley & Sons Canada Ltd.

Library and Archives Canada Cataloguing in Publication

Siskind, Barry, 1946-

    Eagles must soar : 7 simple strategies for living a life with certainty / Barry Siskind.

Includes index.

ISBN 0-470-83468-4

    1. Self-actualization (Psychology)
    2. Certainty.
    3. Uncertainty. I. Title.

BF637.S4S59 2004   158.1   C2004-902931-2

Production Credits:
Cover and Text Design: Ian Koo
Printer: Tri-Graphic Printing Ltd.

Printed in Canada

10 9 8 7 6 5 4 3 2 1

For
Jillian Micole Siskind
and
Geoffrey Brent Siskind

The Eagle's gift of freedom is not a bestowal,
but a chance to have a chance.
———Carlos Castaneda———

CONTENTS

Acknowledgments

I used to think that writing a book meant long solitary hours working on a computer. Now that I've written a number of books I know the whole world is there for me. Getting out in the real world and talking to real people who all seem to be looking for the same thing—a sense that everything will be okay—has been the real motivation behind *Eagles Must Soar*. There are so many people who have offered me their personal anecdotes and suggestions and I am grateful to all of them. I want to particularly thank the folks at Wiley: Karen Milner, Robert Hickey, Megan Brousseau, Terry Palmer and Jennifer Smith. Robert Mackwood, Ken Fisher, Laurie Guttman, Judie Benyei, Andrew Benyei, Joan McKnight, Rabbi Avi Nachmias and the thousands of people who have taken part in my workshops and semi-

Acknowledgments

nars or read my books and have taken the time to share their stories—thank you.

I would also like to thank Geoffrey Siskind, who offered valuable insight and suggestions, and Shawn Mintz, who read an early manuscript and offered his keen feedback.

Special thanks to those who are taking this amazing journey with me including Jillian, Geoffrey, Mark, Robert, Cory, Lynda, Suzanne, Carol, Aidyn, Shawn, Ilmee, Shaindy, Seth, Cheryl, Carl and Esther.

And Barbara: twenty-four years later and we can still surprise each other. It doesn't get cooler than that.

INTRODUCTION

Wherever you go, go there with all your heart.
———— Confucius ————

The eagle represents power, wisdom, courage and freedom. It's no wonder that this magnificent animal has captured the attention of people for ages. It is the focus of folklore and myths throughout most cultures. Ancient carvings of eagles can even be found on cave walls. Why has this one bird captured the imagination of so many? It's not hard to guess. Looking at the eagle floating magnificently across the sky, one sees the ultimate symbol of our certainty. Watching the eagle begs the question "How do I want to live?" Do you want to rank with Teddy Roosevelt's "cold and timid souls" or do you want to soar like an eagle? If it's the latter then keep reading.

Picture your life free from worry. A life as it should be lived, filled with happiness and joy.

"Ahh," you say, "would be nice—but it's a pipe dream. What about terrorists, floods, famine, wars, viruses and all those things I have no control over? Where is this idyllic world now?"

The earth will keep spinning regardless of our best plans. This book offers you an opportunity to find your place in a chaotic world. The strategies in this book promise to make your life as simple as deciding whether you want cinnamon or chocolate sprinkles on your latte, which new movie to see or where to go on your next vacation. Nice way to live, right?

Once you have chosen to live with absolute certainty, this scenario can become reality. There are no more big life-altering choices to make. Just the fun stuff is left. That's what the strategies in *Eagles Must Soar* promise you.

William Shakespeare, Marlon Brando, Mother Teresa, Thomas Edison, Pierre Trudeau and Donald Trump all have something in common? Fame—yes. Respect—yes. Success—yes.

But they also share something else—massive rejection on a scale that would cause many of us to fold. If it were not for Shakespeare's shrewd investments he would have been destined to constantly live one play ahead of poverty. Mother Teresa's struggle to save the poor is legendary. Donald Trump built himself an empire and then it all came tumbling down. Brando, Edison and Trudeau also had their struggles. We all do. All humans struggle. We each have a life path riddled with bumps and roadblocks.

So why, in the face of rejection, did these people persist? The answer is simple. At some level, they knew that beyond talent they needed two things to make everything happen: certainty and common sense.

They needed the certainty that things are unfolding as they should. This means that whatever happened, these people acted to gain value from the experience rather than becoming victims to their circumstances. They needed common sense to recognize and act on these opportunities.

Eagles Must Soar: 7 Simple Strategies for Living a Life with Certainty is about this first need. Herein are seven strategies that will help you develop absolute certainty in your life. The second need, common sense, is covered in my previous book, *Bumblebees Can't Fly: 7 Simple Strategies for Making the Impossible Possible*. In that book, I enlisted other powerful strategies to help the reader find and use common sense.

What Is Certainty?

Certainty is an appropriate topic for our times. When all the signs around us lead to a feeling of uncertainty, knowing that there's an order behind the apparent chaos is essential. In our fast-moving world, focusing on the uncertainties leads to frustration, failure and unhappiness. The more we fail the more failure seems to chase us. It becomes a downward spiral.

So, what is certainty? Philosophers have wrestled with this topic for centuries. The philosopher Edmond Husserl wrote, "Without a basis in some absolute certainty, I cannot live; I cannot bear life unless I can believe that I shall achieve it."

Husserl tried to achieve certainty by explaining human consciousness through scientific means. His most famous protégé, Jean-Paul Sartre, had a different view. Sartre believed human consciousness is individually controlled, not the puppet of exterior forces. Sartre thought we create our own meaning in life. We have the free will to choose how to perceive ourselves and the world. The universe, for Sartre, is a chaotic affair upon which no one can base any sort of certainty.

Which philosopher is right? Both? Or is your certainty based solely on what you can see, touch, smell, taste and feel? Are you certain that your interpretation of those things that you sense is true? Perhaps you base your certainty on one of the great world religions, such as Christianity, Buddhism, Judaism or Islam. Or, perhaps you base your certainty on New Age spirituality. This may take you deep within to an understanding of how it all works and where you belong in the greater scheme.

This book is not about philosophy or religion. It is a practical guide to help you find your own answers to what works for you. You know when you are on the right track, and you feel it in your gut. If you feel discomfort, you know you are heading down the wrong path. So what are you going to do about it? Choose.

Certainty in an Uncertain Age

Our ancestors dealt with different uncertainties. They lived in small villages where their uncertainties were focused on nature: "Will a hurricane wipe us out? Will we find enough food to eat?" However, they had a level of certainty in every other area of life. They knew their place in the family and their role in the village. The rules of behavior were clear and breaking these rules resulted in harsh and immediate punishment. If a villager needed help, then others assisted because they knew that the health of the village depended on the health of its residents.

In today's urban societies, we often don't know our neighbors though they may live on the other side of the fence. If someone is in trouble, it's easier to cast our eyes elsewhere and, like the ostrich, live with our heads in the sand. Consequently, we are skeptical, unbelieving, untrusting and ultimately unhappy.

Life is complicated. We have too many choices and knowing right from wrong is a matter of degrees, carefully scrutinized and determined by lawyers and judges. All the improvement humanity has seen has been at the cost of certainty. A proclamation of certainty in uncertain times almost sounds foolish—yet it's still there, begging to be heard.

With certainty, we are looking at life from an eagle's-eye view, soaring high in the sky and seeing the world as it really is. From this vantage point, we know with absolute certainty that whatever the outcome, the conclusion is the one that works best for us at that time. It's all part of the big, grand plan. People with certainty are like eagles that fly overhead, leaving the rest of us walking in their shadows.

If asked, Brando would have said, "I must act," Shakespeare "I must write," Mother Teresa "I must share," Edison "I must discover," Trudeau "I must lead" and Trump "I must build." They were certain. Somewhere deep in their psyche they knew they were on the right path and, more important, they could not take any other path. They had only one way to go. So, they spread their wings and soared.

Focus on the Journey, Not the Destination

The dictionary defines certainty as the "state of being certain, free from doubt or reservation." But there's more to certainty than just being positive that that our actions will bring us eternal happiness, healthy children, wealth or whatever worldly thing we desire. I'd like to revise the dictionary's definition of certainty to include the following: "Certainty means knowing that everything is going to work the way it should, but not necessarily the way we want." Wanting to achieve particular things focuses us on the wrong place—the goal. *Certainty is not about the destination. It is about the journey.* If we can run our businesses and our lives knowing that we are doing what is right for us—regardless of the outcome—and rid ourselves of the doubt that often holds us back, then our ability to create the right life and business is certain.

If I could visit teenaged William Shakespeare, Marlon Brando, Mother Teresa, Thomas Edison, Pierre Trudeau and Donald Trump and say, "You know, your chances of achieving greatness are very slim. Don't bother trying. Maybe you should get a real job," I assume they all would look at me as if I were an alien. Those people, even when faced with the overwhelming odds, pursued their own paths. They simply did what they must.

George Lucas's film studies professor once told the then budding filmmaker's class, "If any of you want jobs, this is the wrong program." This teacher saw film studies as merely a way for students to avoid the "real world," where they would have to find employment and be productive citizens. But Lucas knew that he had to make films. Did he know that he would go on to make some of the most profitable films in history? Did he dream that he would be one of the most powerful men in Hollywood? Did he think that one day he and his buddies Francis Ford Coppola, Steven Spielberg and Martin Scorsese would change the face of American cinema? I doubt it. All he wanted, and all he ever wants, is to make movies.

We are not like an Olympic athlete who trains for years for the one magical moment of winning gold. In that same competition, many equally deserving athletes are chasing the same reward. If we live our lives like that, all chasing a single goal that only one person can win, then our chances are 98 percent that we will live an unfulfilled existence. It is a recipe for failure and frustration. However, if we can understand how to play the game and relish each moment, then we can all be winners. That's what certainty is all about—making you a winner in the game of life.

The Strategies

As you read *Eagles Must Soar*, you will be taking a journey. The destination doesn't really matter. When you remove uncertainty from your daily life then you can sit back and enjoy the trip. Remember, you only get to take the ride once.

The seven strategies that will guide you to a life and a business filled with certainty are:

Strategy #1: Find the Flow
Understand the natural cycles of everything and know that nothing happens by chance.

Strategy #2: Define Your Certainty
Learn three principles to activate certainty.

Strategy #3: Respect Your Roadblocks
Understand the real role of doubt and fear and develop a five-step proactive approach to overcome them.

Strategy #4: Recognize Your Significance
Move from external motivators to internal motivators.

Strategy #5: Discover Your Purpose
Know what your role is and don't waste valuable energy envying what others have. Stack the odds in your favor.

Strategy #6: Think with Clarity
Eliminate brain clutter and organize your life according to your intention.

Strategy #7: Create Lasting Certainty
Create the small daily steps that will move you in the right direction.

The order of these strategies is important. They represent a step-by-step formula that will change your life and business in ways you never thought possible. At the completion of these steps hope and optimism will have a new meaning. You will feel renewed, refreshed and ready to continue your journey with a different perspective. You will soar with the eagles.

STRATEGY

I

Find the Flow

After all,
tomorrow is another day.
—— Scarlett O'Hara, *Gone with the Wind* ——

"After all, nothing is for certain." Remember that refrain from your childhood? I know I do. When I'd tell my parents of my dreams for glory, they always warned me to have something to fall back on.

Fallback plans make sense in a world filled with uncertainty. How can anyone predict with accuracy how things will work out? That's why as adults, we often push back our lofty dreams and pursue the safety of the fallback position.

A good example of this is my talented friend who, in his early twenties, declared that he wanted to be a writer. He loved writing, had won some prizes and dreamed of writing professionally. His first book of short stories was rejected by dozens of traditional publishers, so he self-published and placed it on consignment in a few bookstores.

Self-publishing meant that my friend was not only the writer of his book, but also its editor, publisher, shipper, salesperson and bookkeeper. It was frustrating. His vision of being the next John Grisham was quickly fading. The message was clear: making a living as a writer was not easy. Still, writing was his passion. A life without writing was not something he wanted, but clearly he needed some options. After all, Grisham had been a lawyer first—right?

My friend decided to attend teachers' college. He could teach and still have time off in the summer to write—the best of both worlds. After graduating, he realized that teaching high school wasn't satisfying enough. Lecturing to university students would be more stimulating. However, to teach at a university required a PhD—seven more years of school! Finally, with his PhD in hand he was ready, but now jobs were scarce. For every interview he went to, another two hundred candidates were vying for the same position. He spent his time writing résumés. When I asked him how his fiction writing was coming along, he replied, "I really don't have time."

My friend had spent the last decade of his young life working on his backup plan. Ten years of minimum wage and long hours at the library and still he had no job in sight.

What happened to my friend happens to many of us: we live the backup plan and pack our dreams away in the attic. Then years later we wonder where the real happiness went. We wake up one day and ask, "What was life all about?" We sense it must be about something more than having a bigger house or better vacations. But, we are not sure.

The same thing can happen to your business. When you created the business, you thought you had something of value to offer. You felt pure joy at coming to work to give life to new opportunities. But only a fortunate few can balance the logistical pressures of running a business with the joy of creating opportunities. The rest of us get caught up in the day-to-day drudgery and lose sight of why we went into business.

What Matters Most?

Why do we let this happen? Common sense plays a role—we're playing it safe. When we put all our eggs in one basket, the risk of failure is greater, although, if you are right, the reward is, too. It's this mixed message that creates uncertainty. Most of us choose practicality and opt not to take that big risk. Only a few of us are willing to become starving artists and commit to the possibility of a lifetime of poverty and sacrifice for our craft. We want other things such as security, comfort and family.

A better approach would be to find a way to live that leaves enough energy for you to have it all. Actors who work nights waiting on tables are an excellent example: waiting does not jeopardize their acting energies. In fact, with the right attitude, it can enhance their acting skills. Waiting on tables is not a backup plan, but a means toward the end. For my friend the writer, teaching should have been a means to the end rather than the end in itself.

You have to decide what matters most. To live life properly is to stay focused. This means doing what you have to do while living the life you want. Easily said, but often hard to do! Priorities change: your health may change, the economic environment will change and family responsibilities will change.

You have a choice. With certainty you can pursue the life you want. Without it, you can scramble for alternatives, live the backup plan or have no plans at all—simply throw your hands in the air, saying, "What's the use?"

The Cycles of Life
I believe that most people fall into a life of uncertainty because they don't understand the cycles

of life. Understanding how to live entails a willingness to move forward with certainty. It means walking the high-wire without a net. High-wire artist Karl Wallenda said, "Being on the tightrope is living, everything else is waiting."

The first step to creating certainty in your life is understanding life's natural cycles. Nothing flows along evenly. When events are at their lowest, this is a clear indication that the high point is just around the corner. Just as in football and soccer, you go along for a while, enjoying a winning streak, but then there is a period where nothing seems to work out. It's when everything turns out wrong that we begin to question the process. As an ancient paradox reads, "Only one thing is certain—that is, nothing is certain. If this is true, it is also false."

Remember the Bible story about Joseph and his ability to interpret dreams? The Pharaoh asked Joseph what his dreams meant and Joseph proclaimed that they foretold seven bountiful years followed by seven years of drought. Although the story doesn't tell us about a third group of seven years, one can assume that the ancient Egyptians could look forward to good times again. During a drought no farmer ever assumes that it will never rain again. Farmers know that nature has cycles. Likewise, economic recessions are preludes to a boom, and the boom is a signal that eventually the bubble will burst. Everything in our world has a natural cycle.

Tom, who is a client of mine, leads his life knowing that things will always work out. Whenever events go wrong, he simply says, "It's for the best." When an opportunity slips through his fingers, Tom tells himself, "When one door closes another opens." Regardless of the situation, he lives with the certainty that everything is going as it should. Is he naive? Does he know something the rest of us apparently don't?

Knowledge vs. Belief

The sun will always rise, but we may not be able to see it because of clouds. Life is like that. It has sunny days and cloudy days. When it's cloudy, we don't say it will never be sunny again. If the weather, history and the economy have a cycle, why should we expect human behavior to be different? It isn't. However, believing in its existence is not enough.

A rabbi once asked me if I believe in God.

"Of course," I answered.

"Well, I don't," he said.

I was floored! How could a man of religion not believe in God? He then explained that he didn't believe there is a God; he *knew* there is. His knowledge of God was unshakeable. This is more than a subtle distinction and it goes to the heart of what certainty is. With certainty, we know that we are on the right course. Belief is really knowledge with an option, like a disclaimer on a product package that reads, "This product may have side effects. If you experience any of these symptoms consult your physician immediately." From an eagle's-eye view, belief's disclaimer is clearly self-imposed. It's as though believers are saying, "If you give me the life I seek or the answer I want, I will believe. If you don't then I have the option of backing out."

As long as that option remains, there is a crack in the foundation, which will allow uncertainty to seep in. The purpose of the journey into certainty is to remove the option.

Watch for the Signs

Knowing about the cycles is the beginning point. It tells you that nothing happens by chance. There is logic to everything, although that logic is often concealed. Once in a while, however, we are given clues—signposts in the cycles. What you need to do is to learn to read these signs.

Imagine you are driving along a country road and you see a sign: "Drive with care, bridge ices quickly." You heed the sign and slow down. As you are crossing, sure enough you hit some ice, but because you were aware you stay in control of your car.

"A good thing the sign was there," you say to yourself. But did that sign appear magically just for you? No, it was always there for any motorist as a warning of potential danger.

Coincidences are like that. They are signs on the highway and are part of the plan. Everyone gets signs. They happen all the time. When you feel crummy and have a headache and a runny nose you know that a cold is on the way. However, you also know that your chances of getting the cold were quite good because a few days ago you attended a parent-teacher meeting where everyone was coughing, sneezing and handshaking throughout the meeting. You will not say, "What a coincidence. I now have the same cold all my friends have."

Doctors understand physical signs and can analyze their possible causes. Police look for signs at a crime scene. Astute business people read the signs of potential business problems. Signs are everywhere and we don't assume they are just co-incidences.

Life has signs for all of us as well. The problem is that we often chalk them up to coincidence. We doubt that what we are exposed to is anything but a freak occurrence without any real meaning. This is often the result of not perceiving life's cycles. Most times these patterns are concealed, but they are there nevertheless. (This concealment is not all bad because when the cycles are hidden, our power of choice is preserved and that is what makes our journey fun!)

Throughout this book you will learn how to read the signs that have been put right in front of you. Your journey into a life of certainty has begun. You know that there are cycles to everything. Where you are now is a prelude to where you will be tomorrow. You also understand that the next phase in the cycle doesn't magically appear, but that there are signs along the road that give you clues to where you are going. With this understanding in place, you are ready to make your quest for certainty a bit more personal.

Creating Certainty from Strategy #1

1. Visit a bookstore or your neighborhood library and go to the biography section. Find an autobiography of some person you have always admired. (I like autobiographies because you are getting the information straight from the horse's mouth, so to speak.) As you read the story, note the cycles of ups and downs experienced by the author. Also, like reading a

good mystery, see if you can find some of the signs that this person might have recognized that were indications of things to come.

2. Now, think about your autobiography. Make a list of your cycles of ups and downs. As you record these changes keep them in chronological order.

3. For the next week, keep a notepad handy and record everything that happens to you that you might normally chalk up to coincidence. At the end of the week, see if some pattern emerges.

STRATEGY

2

Define Your Certainty

I know the price of success:
dedication, hard work
and an unremitting devotion
to the things you want to see happen.
———— Frank Lloyd Wright ————

A woman I know recently had her life changed as a result of a career decision made by her husband. For years he felt unfulfilled in a job that didn't allow him to express a part of him that needed to be heard. Years earlier he had taken a comfortable job that gave him the resources to care for his ailing parents. Now that his parents were gone that need was no longer relevant. His biggest regret was not having attended college. This nagging desire for an education had created an urge that couldn't be ignored. He wanted to experience university as a full-time student, but leaving a comfortable job with a secure pension was difficult. He felt the constraint imposed by his self-locking "golden handcuffs." After many family discussions, they decided to take the plunge. After all, there was no point living a life that was so unfulfilled.

Making a career switch in mid-life can be difficult. For a couple used to a certain standard of living, it can mean a change in financial status. But, somewhere deep within, she knew with certainty that this was the right decision. Years later she freely admits that she "just felt certain" that this would work out for the best. But how did she know? Was she simply naive or perhaps foolish?

This second strategy helps you know where your certainty comes from and how you can engage it in all parts of your life.

We all have moments of certainty. With skill and practice, you can create as many of these moments as you want. Your path is more than a wistful hope for the future: "What will I be?" It is a firm statement of knowledge: "This is how I will live my life." Each of us must choose a path and be secure in the knowledge that it is the right one.

Your Big Choice

I once met a man who was the epitome of pessimism. He was like Eeyore in *Winnie the Pooh*, always finding the gloomy side of things. When we talked, his conversation revolved around how awful his life is, how nobody likes him, how everyone else has everything while he has nothing and on and on.

"What was the highlight of your life?" I asked him.

He looked at me as if I hadn't been listening and said, "My life? Give me a break, nothing ever seems to work out the way it should."

"But there must be some moments, however small, when you felt really positive about things," I countered.

"Like what?" he asked.

I quickly realized this was going to be harder than I thought.

"How about your kids? Your son graduated from engineering school last year. How did you feel when that happened?"

"Great, I know Robbie is on the right tack and has a great life ahead of him."

"Oh, so you feel pretty positive about Robbie, What else do you feel positive about?" He proudly told me about his daughter, who is in nursing school. Then he talked about the woodworking he does in his basement.

"I'd like to see some of the furniture you have made," I said. His face changed before my eyes. For the first time he lost his look of pessimism and smiled.

On a visit to his house to see his wood projects, I asked, "when you start a project do you ever think you will fail?"

"You gotta be kidding," he answered. "I can do this stuff blindfolded. I know exactly what I am doing. When I have a chisel in hand and I'm working on my lathe I know it's going to work out."

We all have moments of certainty like these. The universe flashes them before the pessimist's eyes just to say, "See, this is what life can really be like."

Certainty is within the realm of both the optimist and the pessimist. While each of us has elements of both, we have the power to choose the way we view the world. Why lead a life of doom and gloom when there is an alternative? The purpose of this chapter is to lay the groundwork for you to expand your certainties to include more positive things in your life.

Everyone has a host of certainties. Some yield positive impacts and others negative. As you journey through this book, you will explore the choices you have. My acquaintance Eeyore focused on his negative certainties, overlooking the many positive aspects of his life. Your biggest choice is to focus on positive certainties.

Life is a game, and every game has its winners and losers. When you know for certain the outcome is win or lose, but you can't say for sure which it will be—choose to play the game as if you were a winner. It's your decision, but know that once you choose to live a life of a winner, it is one of the last big choices you will ever have to make.

Filmmaker Federico Fellini said, "Our minds can shape the way a thing will be because we act according to our expectations." If we expect to be winners—if we're certain that we will act successfully—then we've already gone a long way to influencing our path. This is the launching point of your journey into the world of absolute certainty.

Choosing to be a winner affects how we spend the time we have. It goes to the core of who we are and how we act. Do you want to win or lose? Do you want a life with integrity and strong principles? Do you want to leave a lasting mark on those whose path you cross? The answer is clear, but the solution might not be. How can we achieve the certainty of a winner?

The Three Guiding Positive Principles
You don't find certainty—you activate it. Activating it is a matter of letting it breathe. Sometimes it will breathe on its own, while other times we need to apply the defibrillator and give it a spark to correct its fluttering heartbeat.

It's your move. But there are three principles that, if you keep them in mind, will help you to sustain your positive certainty.

#1: Don't Wait for an Epiphany!

An epiphany isn't an event. It is an awakening. Many of us wait for that moment, that one luminous moment when we say, "Aha, I've got it!" That moment is an illusion. It is not really a quantum leap where on one side there is a void and the other side holds the answer. There is no single moment of epiphany that launches us into certainty. However, for many of us, there is a moment when we realize we are already there.

There is a great joke that goes to this very point. A man lived in a home that was threatened by a flood. As the weather worsened, the local police drove up to warn him that he should pack up his belongings and leave. His answer was simply, "God will take care of me."

The weather worsened. The water level rose, so driving his car was no longer possible. State troopers went up and down the streets in motorboats helping stranded residents. When they came to this person, he simply said, "God will take care of me."

Next, the water level got so high that this man was forced up on his roof. A helicopter approached and the Coast Guard beckoned him to grab the ladder so they could take him to safety.

"No thanks," said the man. "God will take care of me."

The waters continued to rise and the man drowned. At the Pearly Gates, he faced God.

"God, what happened? I have always been a pious man. Why didn't you save me?"

God simply looked at the man and said, "How much more do you want from me? I sent the police, the state troopers and the Coast Guard."

Unlike that drowned man, we need to watch closely for the signs that are all around us. We might never get that epiphany—that clear sign from above—so we need to stay positive and pay attention. There's no need to wait until the signs have gathered critical mass; as the drowned man learned far too late, they might not!

I once heard a radio interview with an Anglican minister. His career had led him to a teaching position at a seminary but he was growing increasingly uneasy. He was not getting the response—either professionally or spiritually— that he expected. At one point, he attended an intensive week of Bible study in Los Angeles. Every day he attended theological lectures and every night he took the subway back to his hotel.

Watching the city, he saw neighborhoods, graffiti on the walls, people congregated on the streets. Each evening he saw more. Then, one day, he had his moment of epiphany: what he was learning and ultimately teaching had nothing to do with the people he wanted to serve. This moment changed everything for him. It changed the direction of his ministering forever.

An epiphany is simply a wake-up call to information that is swirling around you waiting to be noticed. It's not that we really ignore this information, we just don't see it for what it is. But if we're positive, and truly optimistic about our prospects in whatever endeavor we take on, we're often more receptive to these signs.

Have you ever been in a situation when you just knew the correct answer to a problem? I don't mean knowing the answer to Regis's question on *Who Wants To Be a Millionaire*? I am not talking about your ability to recall trivia. This is different. It is knowing the right way to deal with your child's behavior or the correct answer to a persistent business problem or the perfect solution to a career challenge. If you can recall one such moment for yourself, see if you can also recall how you felt at that moment. For many, the moment of certainty is one filled with optimism.

When all doubts are erased, regardless of the consequence, there is only one course of action. There is no fear. This was the moment, I am sure, that many of the heroes of September 11 faced. They knew with certainty that the only thing they could do was to rush into the burning building to rescue someone who needed them. When asked about their actions, many heroes replied, "I didn't think about the danger to myself, I just did what I needed to do."

I remember taking my son on a slide ride when he was young. These are giant slides that a ski resort operates in the summer time to attract tourists to their mountain. My son was three or four at the time. He sat in front of me on the sled. As we sped down the slide, we were approached from the rear by a group of people who wanted to go even faster. I held steadfast at a speed I thought was safe and fun for both of us. This wasn't good enough for our tailgaters who then bumped into our sled, causing it to wobble and swerve.

At the bottom of the hill I jumped off my sled and started yelling at these people. In retrospect, this wasn't the smartest course of action. Any one of them could have overpowered me without trouble, but I was like a mother bear protecting her cub. My personal safety didn't matter—only the safety of my child. I knew with certainty at that moment what my job was and what I had to do. At that moment I was fearless, positive and certain.

Was the ride a moment of epiphany? No, it was a reminder of who I really was: a protective father taking care of his offspring. I knew that anytime my children are in danger I will react in such a way. But the sled ride was my wake-up call. It was a glimpse at one certainty that I often took for granted. The good news is that you don't have to wait for a burning building or a threat to your children to know certainty. You have the power to incorporate that same feeling of certainty into every aspect of your life. If you just open your eyes, you'll see that you have clues that disclose your response long before you are actually called upon to act.

Moving from a state of uncertainty to certainty takes time, patience, experience and willingness. Certainty will be an awareness that the right course of action is no longer a choice. It just is. At this point whatever path you choose is the right path; whatever action you choose is the right action.

Your epiphany is the day you wake up and know that you are already there.

#2: Don't Settle for Second Best

Years ago one on my mentors said, "Barry, you can have it all." It took me years to figure out exactly what she meant, but once I did, I knew that it had everything to do with certainty. Certainty is a right, not a gift. It is something we all deserve—if we are truly willing to work for it.

You have all sorts of choices in life. Change your direction and you are on a different path. Life is like that, whether you make the right choice or not is irrelevant—it's simply another direction. Henry Ford said, "Whether you think you can or whether you think you can't, you're right."

If one direction causes you discomfort then change paths once again. You don't have to go anywhere you don't want to go. You don't have to settle for second best—ever. Your journey is what you focus on because that is where your certainty is found. The destination, as you will learn later in this book, may be nothing more than an illusion.

#3: Don't Let Others Determine Your Certainty

Now here is a tough one. As a father and stepfather, one of the most difficult things for me to accept is that my adult children have everything they need, in spite of me. They need my love as I need theirs. When they need my guidance, they will ask for it. I've come to learn that helping someone who doesn't want it or isn't ready causes problems.

It's like the story of the Boy Scout who helps a blind man cross the street. The blind man struggles, but the Boy Scout is determined to do his good deed. At the other side of the street the blind man yells at the Boy Scout. The Boy Scout is shocked.

"Look. I helped you cross the street. The least you can do is stop yelling and say thanks," he tells the blind man.

"But now," says the blind man, "I have to get back to the other side because that's where I am being picked up."

My job as a parent is to sit back and watch my children choose their own paths. Sometimes things are going to work and sometimes they won't. Every decision will provide them with powerful life lessons and prepare them for their unique futures.

Knowing I can't do more than this for my children also says that nobody can do more for me. My path is my path. Nobody has the right to tell me I'm on the wrong path (assuming that what I am doing is legal!). When others observe my actions and see mistakes, I see lessons. When they see successes, I also see lessons. Nobody can be in my skin, experiencing my feelings and thinking my thoughts. Nobody can determine my certainty. Only I can do it for myself.

Being Sure About Certainty

Let's take a moment to recap. So far you have learned that each of us is a player in a game. The obvious outcomes to that game are winning or losing and there are no guarantees which it will be. Therefore, focusing on the outcome cannot lead to certainty.

All you can do, with certainty, is choose how you want to play the game. You can play as a winner or a loser. It's your choice. There are three guiding principles that will help you keep a positive spirit: don't wait for epiphanies, don't settle for second best and don't let others determine your certainty. Now you are ready for the next strategy on the road to certainty, which will teach you how to handle the roadblocks.

Creating Certainty from Strategy #2

1. On a sheet of paper, draw three columns. In the first column, make a list of those things of which you are certain. This is your list, so no matter how trivial the item seems, write it down.

2. For each item, ask yourself, "When did I first know I was certain about this?" Write the answers in the second column.

3. In the third column, list any clues or signs that you can recall that predate the time you actually became aware of your certainty.

STRATEGY

3

Respect Your Roadblocks

The only limit to our realization
of tomorrow will be our doubts of today.
——— Franklin Delano Roosevelt ———

The road to certainty is strewn with roadblocks. Unlike a real highway, though, these obstacles in your path don't need to cause detours or long delays. The roadblocks on this highway are actually an integral part of life and can have positive effects on everything you do. Each roadblock is really a chance to learn more about your chosen path and help define your journey.

A few years ago, I invested a lot of time and energy in a business deal that fell apart. I was devastated and searched for an answer as to why I'd failed. Recently, a contact that I had made during that apparent business fiasco came to me with a tremendous proposal. The implications of this were far greater than my original business. If I had been saddled with the original, I would have missed this new opportunity. My roadblock actually led me to another road that was even better. Was I just lucky or was something else going on?

Voltaire wrote, "Luck is a word devoid of sense; nothing can exist without a cause." My luck was a result of a missed opportunity. Looking back, I realize that there were many signs that the first deal would have never worked. Had I read those signs at the time, I would have been able to sidestep the deal's demise. This proactive approach would have allowed me to take control earlier; my actions would have made me a roaring success. Be proactive and take control: that is the underlying lesson you will learn in this strategy.

Detained by Doubt

Picture your world as a horizontal line. At one end you have certainty. This is a place where you know that each action you take is right for you. Here, you play the game as a winner and feel comfortable within your own skin.

At the opposite end of the line lies uncertainty. This is the place of hesitancy, tension and fatigue. Here, you are a victim to the ebbs and flow of life.

Uncertainty ———————————— Certainty
Doubt

When you look at this line, there is no obvious connection between certainty and uncertainty. You are at one side or the other. When you are uncertain, you are uncertain, period. And when you are certain, you are certain. Some certain people experience moments of uncertainty and, conversely, uncertain people have moments of certainty.

What stops you from free-flowing back and forth across this path are roadblocks that take the form of doubt. Doubt can change your course.

We all go along in life knowing everything is going as it is supposed to—then doubt rears its ugly head. But doubt is merely a messenger and is not always a bad thing. These visitations by doubt can be momentary glimpses into what is possible or a cloud that casts its shadow on everything we do. Once you understand what doubt is, you can put it in its place.

In Strategy #2, I talked about my acquaintance who was offered moments of certainty through his children and his carpentry. For the uncertain person like him, these moments of certainty are clues offered by the universe of what is possible.

For the certain person, doubts serve the same function as those moments of certainty for uncertain people. A moment of doubt offers a reality check. It's an opportunity to refocus on a more satisfying way of living.

Doubts are devious characters. On one hand they can trigger a downward spiral of uncertainty that gains momentum if things are not brought into check quickly. William Shakespeare wrote, "Our doubts are traitors, and make us lose the good we oft might win, By fearing to attempt." The astute observer, however, knows that doubt's other face is one of opportunity.

But to truly understand our doubts and turn them into opportunities, we need to look at them more closely. Doubts don't just happen. There has to be a cause.

Fear

Doubt is really a reaction to fear. Although doubt and fear are closely related, there are differences. Fear is an emotional reaction based on real or illusionary stimuli. Doubt, on the other hand, is a response tied directly to what we are afraid of. Doubt creates the action (or inaction). Doubts often are heard through those nagging messages we give ourselves that are a direct result of a fear. Without fear there would be no doubt. Without doubt, fear would have no way of expressing itself.

If you're afraid of rejection, fear can stop you from taking risks. The fear of reprisal may stop you from suggesting good ideas and so on. These are merely excuses for inaction. When you give this much power to fear, you become its victim. The tighter its hold, the more difficult it is to escape.

On the other hand, fear can also be a tremendous motivator. My fear of failure motivates me to work the long hours it takes to be successful. My fear of not being the kind of boss I want to be motivated me to try harder with employees.

Fear has a place. It is a part of you to be honored. You have fears for a reason. Understanding your fear's underlying purpose is more useful than trying to eliminate it from your life. Your fear is actually an opportunity to know yourself better and more freely. When we know our fears, we can choose what to do with them. If they are debilitating and get in the way of our life, professional help is in order. More often than not, though, we can find a way of dealing with them ourselves.

There are three types of fear. There are our fears of things over which have no control, such as aging, dying or getting sick. Next, there are our fears that are prompted by an impending action on our part. This action could be a decision to return to school, change careers or end a relationship. Finally, there are the fears that come from the inner states of our minds—our egos. These fears are manifested in concerns about rejection, success, failure, being vulnerable, being conned and feeling helpless.

Whether the fear is the result of an external stimulus or generated internally, the real question is, what is its purpose?

As I mentioned earlier, I have a fear of failure. When I was in my twenties it looked and felt as if my future was secure. I had a great job, new family, home in the suburbs, a mortgage, a dog, all the trappings of growing success. I was invincible, master of my own universe or so I thought. Then I hit thirty. I was now divorced and bankrupt. No career, no family, no job, so my search began. I tried a number of things and then one day I knew in my head (and heart) what I could do—teach. I was a teacher. I taught night school classes while I was at university and really loved the experience.

On one hand, I felt a strong pull toward teaching and wanted to start my own training company. On the other hand, my fear of failure said, "What if you blow it?" It was like the cartoon where a man has an angel on one shoulder, a devil on the other, each whispering a different message into the man's ears. I remember driving home one day saying to myself, "Blow it here and you are going to end up working for someone else, doing something you don't really like just for a paycheck." This was not how I wanted to live my life.

My fear of failure motivated me. I remember that day as clearly as if it were today. The fear scared me so much that I swore never to fail again. For me fear was an opportunity to know myself. There is no need to fear your fears. They are an important part of you; they make you who you are.

Doubts and their underlying causes, fears, are two of the signs on our highway. When we read them properly, they lead us to a greater understanding of who we are.

Five Steps to Facing Your Fears and Doubts

We don't want to get rid of fear or doubts, we just want to learn how to keep them in their place and to make them work for us. The Tibetan word *rewa* is the word for hope and the word *dokpa* means fear. The word *re-dok* is a combination of the two, a two-sided equation of hope and fear. Looking for the hope in your fears and doubts is sometimes a challenge but it is always there.

Harnessing the real power of doubt and its underlying motivator, fear, is possible. Instead of choosing to be a reactive victim of fear, relinquishing your power to circumstances, you can be proactive and create certainty in any situation.

You bring proactivity into your life with the following five steps.

#1: Stop

Whoa! Stop that galloping horse before it gets out of control. It doesn't really matter what those mutterings in your brain are all about, so long as you stop them. Obviously, the sooner you stop the messages, the easier you're able to control the situation. The longer you leave it the greater the risk of a stampede. The more you practice these five steps the better you get at recognizing the signs early.

We all give ourselves clues that tell us how we are handling doubt. It could be anger, disappointment, frustration, surprise or confusion. We might lash out and scream or quietly withdraw. We may feel defensive and start making all sorts of excuses. Whatever your mode of operation, it is important to recognize how you handle doubt.

This is tough and requires training. Think of yourself like a fine automobile. As you drive you emit certain noises that let your driver know everything is all right. When the sound changes, your driver immediately knows something is wrong and checks under the hood. Then if he finds a loose fan belt or the engine not working at capacity, he can take you in for repair. The more you are aware of the sounds you make in your mind the more you are aware of changes. These changes are the messages that indicate something is different and it's time to check under your own hood.

#2: Pause and Replay

Replay that inner message. Listen carefully to what it's saying. If you can hear it, write the message down. As an impartial observer, look at the words. Use your eagle's-eye perspective.

Ask yourself, "How does this message affect my feelings of certainty?" You know what it feels like when you are certain, so as you listen to the message, what has changed for you? How are these messages different from the messages you give yourself when you are in a state of certainty?

Ask yourself a series of questions about the message—find the problem. Don't attack the doubt; rather, study it to see if you can find out what it is trying to tell you.

Then ask yourself, "Is this who I really want to be?" This is a difficult one. Picture the type of person you want to be and ask yourself if this message is consistent with that image. When you are faced with doubts and hear the mutterings of your mind, ask yourself if what you're hearing is really you. Do you really want to be grumpy, angry or bitchy? Is that who you really want to be? The answer is invariably no.

#3: Uncover the Fear

The result of your analysis should reveal the heart of the problem—your fear. Some fears are rational. If you doubt whether you should jump out of an airplane with a parachute that you packed yourself—and you have never had a lesson on packing a parachute from a professional—then your fear of dying is probably realistic. This doubt is founded in reality. Here, your doubt is telling you to rethink this particular action.

When your fears are founded in irrational things, like my fear of failure was, then seeing the root of your fear gives you a chance to do something about it. You can live your life as a victim of fear or take control.

As Sir Ernest Shackleton set out on his Antarctic mission, this message was loud and clear. Shackleton ran into barriers throughout the planning process in the form of skeptics.

"Do you really think you can do this?" the skeptics asked him.

"Yes," Shackleton replied emphatically. He had no doubt about the success of his mission. Later, he met with the king of England who, as they said farewell, asked Shackleton, "Do you feel fear?"

Shackleton turned, faced the king and simply said, "Yes."

We all have the power to feel the doubt and remain frozen, or face the fear and move on.

#4: Thank Your Doubt

The next step is the realization that you have been given a gift, an opportunity to grow. That's what doubts are all about—a chance to discover parts of you that need some attention. Doubts, like roadblocks, force you to stop in your tracks and examine alternate courses of action. If you ignore the doubts, you can end up on a rough road. If you listen and deal with them properly, then you can look forward to a much more comfortable trip.

The obvious next action is one of politeness. Anyone who gives you a gift of value deserves your gratitude. Thanking the roadblock for the message is more than an idle statement; it is a strong affirmation that you really understand its value. This may sound absurd. How can you be happy when you have reached a roadblock? But the roadblock is really an opportunity for necessary self-examination. That is one of the greatest gifts of all. It will help you make the next part of your trip smoother.

#5: Action

Here is the test. Take action. The challenge is balancing two opposing forces: your mind, which says one thing, and your gut, which says another. This is normal. It takes time for the two to work in harmony. Be proactive and take action anyway.

These five steps will lead you in the right direction to proactively moving over the road-blocks. But, if you don't feel certainty yet, don't let the lack of feeling inhibit your actions. As Oliver Wendell Holmes Jr. said, "When in doubt, do it." That's right, fake it!

Changing behaviors is not easy and certainly not instantaneous. It requires learning new ways of doing things. New skills take time to integrate into your being. So, for now, proceed as if you were already there. You will be amazed at the speed at which your knowledge will catch up with your actions.

Life is actually very good. It can be a win-win game once you understand that those things in your path are actually there to smooth out the journey for you. With this realization, you are taking important steps in creating a life of certainty. Next, take your search one step further as you explore your significance.

Creating Certainty from Strategy #3

1. Recall the last time you had doubts. You may remember a gnawing feeling in your gut, a lack of desire, and a resistance to try something

new or even shame and embarrassment. Write down the messages you gave yourself when you were in this state.

2. Take these messages and write out the scenario in as much detail as possible. This "writing out" often gives you important clues to the underlying fears that were triggered.
3. With the gift of hindsight, relive this situation, using the five steps. What actions would you take?

STRATEGY

4

Embrace Your Significance

Everyone who got where he is
had to begin where he was.
———— Richard L. Evans ————

We all like to know that what we do with our life matters. Sometimes our efforts are rewarded with money, prizes and possessions. Other times, we receive intangible rewards, such as love, respect and recognition. Regardless of the reward, we're often left wanting more: a need to know that we are significant. This ultimate reward is not automatically given. It has to be earned.

A friend and fellow author once had a dispute with his publisher. He had written a terrific book and wanted to work closely with his publisher to bring it to market. He met with his publisher to discuss promotion ideas. Out of every fifteen ideas he presented, only one was followed through. Time and again my friend would call up the publisher and ask what was happening with all his other ideas. Finally, the frustrated publisher said, "Listen, your book is only one of seventy we are trying to promote." What a reality check for my friend. This comment cut like a knife into the heart of his significance. It was as though a bright, brilliant star suddenly realized that the sky is filled with billions of other stars, just like him.

My friend persevered and said, "But my book is different. It is going to be your next bestseller." Every author likely says the same thing, and the bottom line is that while my friend was certain, his publisher wasn't. The harsh reality is that my friend hadn't earned his publisher's certainty. When John Grisham wants some attention, everyone listens. Why? Because he earned his significance. How? Money, volume and ability to attract media. Significance is not a right; it is a gift that we give ourselves through hard work. In this strategy you will learn about your significance and the principles you need to master to earn it.

Achievement: The Measure of Significance?

Most of us consider the world's significant people to be those who have achieved greatness. But when a person's significance is determined by achievement, it's a recipe for disappointment. The net result of a lifetime is often brought down to success or failure, and nothing in between. Success is often nothing more than a milestone with nothing beyond—nothing to motivate you to the next step. The actor Billy Bob Thornton asked, "Do I want my tombstone to only read, 'He made some movies'?"

Life isn't always kind. Often we have obstacles thrown on our path to test our mettle. One such obstacle is failure. When we base significance on achievement, failure is always waiting to jump out and hit us on the head. Failure has a negative connotation. It can harm your sense of worth. It can attack your sense of significance. Failure can be painful, embarrassing and humiliating. It can permanently derail anyone. But failure can also have a positive purpose. On the *Tonight Show*, author James Carvelle asked fellow guest Robin Williams, "How many jokes have you told that didn't work?" Williams simply said, "How much time do you have?"

When I drive home, I pass one of Canada's premier thoroughbred nurseries. I often stop and gaze at these magnificent horses. Thoroughbred horses are bred to win. Horses like Man of War, Secretariat and Northern Dancer have become legends as a result of their accomplishments on the track. Before each race, these horses are exercised to limber up. Then they are deprived of their morning oats and hay so that by race time their stomachs are empty. This "drawing-up" of the horses' stomachs is important because digesting uses energy that needs to be spent on the race. Their water intake is also reduced to just enough to keep them hydrated. Once the race is completed, the victorious horse goes to the winner's circle with his owners for awards, photographs and accolades. The losers go back to the stable where they can dive into their missed breakfast.

Now, if you were the horse, where would you rather be? In the winner's circle or having your overdue breakfast? Who is the real winner in a horse race? It's all about your perspective. It means understanding the true purpose of your supposed failure.

People with certainty understand failure and can deflect harm with their protective shield. This shield is the knowledge that everything happens for a reason. Every joke that didn't work brought Robin Williams closer to the jokes that did. The person with certainty understands that nothing is coincidental. Everything has a purpose—even failure. In his autobiography, Walt Disney wrote, "One of the best things that happened to me was a bankruptcy at an early age." While the bankruptcy surely was painful, he came through the experience and blossomed.

If you feel certain inside, then you are okay no matter what the world throws in your direction. True significance is generated internally. As you learned in Strategy #3, the obstacles or failures you face are gifts of your fears

The Big Deal About Small Acts

The reality is that we are all significant. Every action is connected. Bill and Melinda Gates can give away $24 billion to help bring better health care to children, but does an act of that magnitude have more significance than a small act of kindness to a stranger? No.

Ivan Vaughan and Jacob Einstein both have something in common. They did small acts that affected our view of the world. Significance comes from these small acts. Ivan Vaughan was a friend of Paul McCartney who invited Paul to hear The Quarrymen play in 1957. One member of The Quarrymen was Ivan's buddy John Lennon—and the rest is history.

Jacob Einstein lent a book of algebra to his nephew who had just entered the Luitpold Gymnasium in Munich. His nephew's education focused on Latin and Greek rather than mathematics and science, so Jacob taught his nephew how to approach algebra as a game. In his later life, young Albert Einstein used his uncle's approach in his work. The rest is history.

Every day, small acts can have significance beyond our imagination. If we knew the magnitude of the impact some of our small acts of kindness have, we'd be speechless. In Frank Capra's movie *It's a Wonderful Life*, his hero, George Bailey (played by James Stewart), relives his life with the help of an angel named Clarence. As George slowly realizes that his life has significance, he says, "Strange, isn't it? Each man's life touches so many other lives, and when he isn't around he leaves an awful hole, doesn't he?" George had changed the course of history for many of the people in the town. Without his presence the world would have been a very different place. We're all like George Bailey.

I saw an advertisement for an organization called the Corporate Angel Network. This is a group of fifty-six of the Fortune 100 companies that have one thing in common—corporate jets. These jets, which crisscross the globe daily carrying executives from one meeting to the next, are often not filled to capacity. Hence the Corporate Angel Network. It coordinates these empty seats and arranges passage for cancer patients. A small thing, but nevertheless, with one flight here and one flight there, suddenly they can boast more than 14,000 free trips for cancer patients.

Whether you share your corporate jet or teach a kid how to hold a baseball bat, your actions are significant. It's like the butterfly that flaps its wings, causing a tornado on the other side of the planet. We are all significant. The smallest acts puts into motion a force that has endless repercussions.

The True Measure of Significance

Significance and certainty go hand in hand. If you've based your entire self-image on big business successes, you're taking a giant risk. Fortunes can fall all too quickly. But if you look at the big picture, and realize that, like George Bailey, actions that seem inconsequential to you can mean the world to someone else, your whole sense of your own significance can change. Your eagle-eye's view of the world leads to a new way to consider significance.

If power, recognition and achievement aren't the true measure of our significance, what is? Humility, sharing, surrender, compassion, hope and an understanding of everything we have and are: that's what truly makes us significant. If we define significance under those terms, we're the judges of our own importance, and therefore we can be far more certain of ourselves. Instead of measuring ourselves by outside standards, striving for hollow goals, we can operate from our hearts. Only then will we understand our true significance.

Humility

A rabbi once spoke to a group of over-achievers—men and women who had built successful companies and considerable personal wealth before they reached forty. As he addressed this group of hotshots he told them about the power of prayer and its real purpose. In the Jewish tradition, there are many prayers that all start the same way: "Blessed art thou, Oh Lord our God, ruler of the universe who brings forth. . . ." The purpose of these prayers, according to the rabbi, is a reality check. Can any of us make food out of nothing, make the sun rise or ensure everlasting love? We are an important part of the bigger picture, but we are not omnipotent. We need to understand that each one of us is only one player on the chessboard. As much change as our actions bring, others bring about an equal amount of change.

For many of us in the "Me Generation," we were the center of the universe. We were like Sherman McCoy, the hero in Tom Wolfe's *The Bonfire of the Vanities*, who was a self-proclaimed "master of the universe." However, the realization that we are a small, and yet significant, part of the larger picture, puts our importance in perspective.

Sharing

After September 11, American music and film stars got together and put on a telethon to raise much-needed money. Average people pledging $5 or $10 together raised more than $1 billion. That's sharing!

Although sharing is innate, this principle takes sharing one step further. We don't need a major catastrophe to awaken our ability to share. Sharing is something that happens every day.

The Hebrew word *tzadaka* means sharing. *Nedava*, a closely related word, means generous. Yet there's a difference between the two. With *tzadaka*, there is no choice—one must share—but *nedava* implies selection—one chooses to be generous. *Tzadaka* is a responsibility. Young Jewish children are taught that the gift of a few pennies here and there, or sharing joy with those who need their smile, is something they must do—not out of generosity but because it's what they must do.

Sharing can include dropping a few coins into a collection box, holding the door open for someone who needs help, mentoring or volunteering in your community. There is no limit to the inventory of sharing opportunities. To share is to be a significant human being.

Surrender

Before we can achieve true certainty, we must give up goals that are fraught with uncertainty. Only then can we reach a point where we can say, "This is the kind of life I want to live."

There is a Tibetan word, *ye tang che*. *Ye* means "totally or completely" and the rest means "exhausted." Together *ye tang che* describes the experience of giving up. This is an important point that we must reach in order to become the people we are to become. The Zen monk Ryokan said, "If you want to find the meaning, stop chasing after so many things. Your significance is found when you surrender those goals that you thought were so significant and accept who you are and what you have to give."

Compassion

From the vantage point of the eagle, high in the sky, everything in the landscape has an important role. The trees, animals, rivers and oceans are an integral part of the whole. Your compassion starts with an understanding that everyone is on an important journey. Rather than looking down on the homeless or being impatient with employees who "just don't get it," we need to look at everyone with an open heart. We need to understand that they have a critical part to play.

Mother Teresa said, "If you judge people, you have no time to love them." Compassion is not pity. It understands the importance of all people in the big picture. Compassion puts your significance into perspective.

Our Significant Realization

As we watch TV shows and read articles that celebrate the great wealth and accomplishments of the rich and famous, it's easy to get caught up in those material things and impressive feats and think that's what's significant. But when we take a step back, it's quite clear that real significance isn't measured externally, but internally. True significance lies in our humility, sharing, surrender and compassion. If we give freely of ourselves, shake off our misguided goals and see that everyone is important and worthy, we'll find that we feel much more significant and certain of ourselves. We won't be waiting to see if we've won the game—we'll know that we've played like winners.

Embracing your significance is the first of a three-part plan. The next question is "What is your purpose?" This is followed by the all-important question "What is your intention?"

Creating Certainty from Strategy #4

1. Think of a time when you acted like a real jerk. It could have been a situation with your family, friends or colleagues. Pick a time when you felt embarrassed or ashamed of the way you handled a situation. Recall this experience in as much detail as possible and write it down strictly from your point of view.

2. Now say to yourself, "Okay, I was a jerk— what did I learn from this situation?"

3. Think the situation through from the perspectives of the other people who were involved. Find one positive thing that you learned from each person.

4. Think about the principles from Strategy #4. How do they effect the way you look at this situation?

STRATEGY

5

Discover Your Purpose

You must do what you must do.
——— Martin Luther King Jr. ———

"What is my purpose?" It's a big question we all wrestle with at one time or another.

Some of us are lucky. From an early age, some fortunate souls have a clear sense of their significance and purpose. For others, the late bloomers, a purpose emerges as they age. Then there is a third group that struggles and searches for a purpose, never seeming to find it. They often unknowingly walk right by it. This strategy is all about helping you set up the right environment so that when you and your purpose cross paths, you won't walk on by your purpose you will stop and embrace it.

Employ Your Eagle Eye

There is a field of sunflowers where I live. When the sunflowers are in bloom, they stand four to six feet tall. Thousands of sunflowers standing side by side, like rows of soldiers with their faces turned to the sun. When the wind blows, the sunflowers move in harmony. They gently sway to the left then the right, responding instantly to the changing late-summer breezes.

Passing motorists stop and take pictures as they try to capture the moment. The field is what it was meant to be. Each sunflower plays an integral role; if one sunflower has not blossomed fully, it disrupts the whole field. One black face stands out like a blemish on this otherwise perfect picture. On first glance we have a multitude of identical sunflowers, but this is an illusion. Not all sunflowers are identical. Some are small and some are big. Some have numerous seeds in their centers. Some have few. But, in spite of their differences, each sunflower is necessary. Each sunflower plays a role in making this field such a beautiful sight.

Each one of us is like the sunflower. We have an important place in the field of life. Imagine that an extraterrestrial being is observing life on earth. To this being all earthlings look the same. Some lighter and others darker, some tall and others short, but basically, like the sunflowers in the field, we look all the same. We earthlings would be observed going about our daily lives governed by our own late-summer breezes that move us to and fro. From this unique vantage point, the observer with his eagle-eye's perspective sees the patterns of humanity.

But here we stand right in the heart of the action. From our narrow vantage point we can differentiate one human being from the next. More often than not, our perceptions and reactions of others are based on these differences. We compare the obvious physical differences, and differences that aren't immediately apparent, like our accomplishments.

Some people will accumulate huge reserves of wealth, fame, notoriety, love or respect. Often these individuals who have accomplished extraordinary success become role models that we strive to emulate. We mistakenly assume that if we mimic their actions or buy the products they endorse we can be more like them and can be as famous and as beautiful as Julia Roberts, as smart as Albert Einstein or as rich as Bill Gates. But looking at our purpose in the shadow of their accomplishments is to base our purpose on ego. Then when we fail to measure up we blame the universe or ourselves for their imperfections. It's like the sunflower saying it wants to be the tallest in the field. When the other flowers overshadow it, the ambitious one says, "This field sucks!" This ego-based approach to purpose wastes our precious time on earth.

Bill Gates has accumulated a fortune worth tens of billions of dollars. Coveting that accomplishment or creating it as your goal is like buying a ticket on the lottery. Fat chance. It's easy to purchase a ticket on any of a number of lotteries with an investment of a dollar or two where your chances of winning the jackpot are 20 million to one. But, in the history of the world, there have been billions of people and only one hit Bill Gates's jackpot. Are you prepared to bet your whole life that you can win the Gates Prize as well? Just think of the odds. There is no certainty in unrealistic notions.

It's time to get with the program. Our space visitor has a unique advantage—detachment. He can take a cold, hard and dispassionate look at the big picture. The extraterrestrial stands back and sees that each person contributes to the whole. Like a professional sports team, we work best when every player is in top form. One injury will affect the whole team. Each of us can also look with detachment from our eagle-eye perspective. But seeing the big picture does not mean that your purpose will jump out and bite you on the ankle. This detachment from your everyday dealings just gives you a more honest look at yourself and an understanding of how you fit in. Mourning Dove, a Salish native said, "Everything on the earth has a purpose, every disease and every person a mission." The next four steps will guide you to the clues to uncover one of your life's greatest mysteries—your purpose.

Confront the Unknown

In the previous strategy you learned to stop measuring your significance through external benchmarks: your true significance comes from within. You accomplished this by focusing on the little things that you normally take for granted. But if you leave your journey there, you'll be facing the unknown without any sense of purpose. We need purpose; without it, we wander aimlessly from one thing to the next, accomplishing nothing.

This unknown can invoke fear and uncertainty. Within it, you might feel disoriented and confused. All your senses might cry out to fill that void with something familiar, and you might be tempted to reach for the illusory goals we abandoned in the last strategy—just to avoid facing the unknown. As Leo Buscaglia wrote, "We all fear what we don't know—it's natural."

Imagine the crew of Christopher Columbus's three ships as they left for their journey to Asia. Collective wisdom said then that the world was flat, and if you traveled long enough you would eventually fall over the edge. This crew had embarked on a journey into the unknown. The lure of wealth, their sense of adventure and their awareness of their purpose drove them on. Somehow a future filled with fame, fortune and accomplishment was a far greater motivator than the relative risk of perishing by falling off the edge of the world. Like Columbus's crew, we have a choice: we can live in uncertainty, embracing illusions, or we can confront the unknown and find our certainty.

Your future exists only in your imagination. You can't skip to the end and peek at the last chapter. You must live life chapter by chapter and wait for the story to unfold. Every day you face the unknown and wonder, "How will this day turn out? Will a tornado wipe out all my possessions? Will I be fired? Will I get the raise? Will my kids arrive for dinner on time?" The best you can do is to be willing to enter the unknown with your eyes and heart open. Experience the world as it unfolds around you. As Thomas Fuller wrote, "He that fears not the future may enjoy the present."

I remember times sitting at my parents' dining room table hearing stories about my ancestors and their accomplishments. One story was about a relative who made and lost fortunes. He would buy a house and move his whole family in, remodel and then sell it for a small profit. He would do this over and over again, and eventually he accumulated a large fortune—to hear my family tell it, at one point, my ancestor owned New Jersey. Then through bad luck he lost it all.

There was another relative who lost a farm to taxes. The location is now a busy downtown corner in Toronto. Today, that property is worth millions. Other lives were summed up in a single line. "He was the one who wrote a best seller; she was married five times; he spent time in jail; she was arrested in a feminist march."

Think about some of your ancestors. What do you remember about them? Have their lives been distilled into a single line? Surely they did more, but the hard truth is that in a few generations one line might be all they say about you, too.

So, let's take control of the future and write our own epitaph. What do you want them to say as they sum up your life? It's not a simple task, but focusing on the question will help you confront the unknown.

It's your future. You decide. But unless you are willing to take the chance and embrace the unknown, you will only be an observer on this wonderful voyage of life. Accepting the unknown opens a world of discovery and new possibilities as you move toward your purpose. It is a crucial step toward living every day with certainty.

Live with the Enigma

It is often assumed that asking questions is the first part of the exercise to finding your self's purpose. In our gigahertz society we have come to expect immediate answers. Having no foreseeable answer can lead to confusion and anger. This is the dilemma politicians face daily. If they choose to act on an initiative with clearly defined objectives that can be accomplished in a finite amount of time, they stand a good chance of staying in power. Politicians who implement initiatives with long-range solutions and outcomes that are difficult to measure face the wrath of voters.

The greatest thinkers of all time have asked important questions and then spent their lives pondering the answers. Stephen Hawking's quest for the unified theory of the universe is one amazing example. His life is spent playing with ideas as a child would play on a sandy beach. He's not sure what to make of his pile of sand but knows that the real joy is in the play. Ultimately he may get his sandcastle built before the waves wash it away.

These questions are not just reserved for intellectuals like Stephen Hawking, however. They provide all of us with the motivation for the journey. Our purpose is often revealed through these big questions that cause us to step back from the crossed t's and dotted i's of our daily lives and to view the world from an eagle's-eye perspective.

The trick is to ask the questions and be prepared to live with the enigma until the answers appear. Appreciate the joy of thinking of the questions in the first place. "Can I be remembered as a great musician? Can I build a business that will last for generations? Can I ingrain lasting values in my family? One question often opens Pandora's box to a million more. The more you ponder, the more questions will appear.

These questions that lead you to your purpose often emerge spontaneously. You will be sitting in a busy mall and might wonder, "What's this really all about?" Perhaps in your car you'll ask, "What's the rush?" In the middle of the night you might awake with a burning desire to know if you are on the right track. Record these questions as they appear. Keep the list by your bedside table, your computer or wherever you can reach it easily. As new questions emerge, write them down.

Visit your list regularly, and you will find a few amazing things. The first is that some questions are really not worthy of your attention. Often, when you read over your list after some time, you shake your head and wonder why you ever spent time worrying about that particular item at all. It may have seemed important at the time but in hindsight, and with detachment, it really wasn't. That's okay. It's better to write all the questions down and revisit them later. Analyzing them as you go often stifles the creative process you are trying to engage.

You'll also find questions on your list that are easily answered. "Am I really loved?" To get this answer, simply go out and ask the people you care about. They will tell you that you are loved. "Can I learn how to play the guitar?" A few lessons and some practice will soon let you know. These questions are easy and can be dealt with quickly. Now you are left with the really worthwhile questions.

Joan Baez once said, "As long as one keeps searching, the answers will come." The answers may not be apparent at first, but with some time and thought, you will condense your list to those questions that are worth investing your life answering. With this shortlist you can begin the process of looking for true answers. After a while you will discover that there's a pattern to your questions—an invisible thread that joins them.

Having questions with no immediate answer may seem counter-intuitive in our "quick-fix" society. Accepting this enigma is the only way to let these answers find you.

Welcome Your Predisposition

Quincy Jones loves music and music defines who he is. It guides his life and business. Stephen Hawking loves science. Stephen King loves writing. My dad loved his family. Mother Teresa loved helping. What's true for exceptional people like these is true for us all: each of us has a predisposition. Those who lead lives of quiet desperation have simply not found (or acknowledged) their calling.

Imagine visiting the General Motors factory and watching them grind out car parts: brakes, filters, taillights, engines, seats and directional signals. A whole bunch of individual parts uniquely designed to make the car work. A tailpipe is a tailpipe and there is no use trying to make it act like a windshield. We are like that. Goethe wrote, "If God had wanted me otherwise, He would have created me otherwise." We are built for our purpose.

We are all made differently. We have different skills, aptitudes and abilities. Some of us have a body type that gives us an advantage as dancers. Other people have an innate ability to paint, while still others can pick up any musical instrument and play it. It's up to each one of us to find out what we were made for.

It's easy to be seduced by a fantasy that looks breathtaking but is not for you. You might say,

"I'd like to be as rich, famous and talented as Tiger Woods." This is a daydream. There are only a select number of contenders to his crown. Do you really have what it takes to join that elite group of individuals? Fantasies have to be kept in their place. They are not part of the real world. Sir Walter Raleigh knew his limitations when he wrote, "I can't write a book commensurate with Shakespeare, but I can write a book by me."

The clues the real world offers us about our predispositions are often not glamorous. They are usually mundane. A successful sculptor I know is also an engineer who, before becoming a full-time artist, worked for a large utility company. He now tells stories of presentations he made where he joyfully dressed up his slides with hand-drawn cartoons. A career civil servant I know had a life-long interest in hockey and children. Now he can be found coaching junior hockey. A third friend spent her life organizing things such as trade shows, conferences and Christmas parties for corporations. She is now the executive director of a local theater group.

You can ignore the clues but they will not go away. Your real predisposition will keep coming back time and time again, like a persistent neighbor you try to avoid, until you finally listen.

You might think that your common sense is telling you to ignore your predisposition. Let me explain. Let's say you have a passion for bicycling. You might acknowledge that you have the right body, have always loved the sport and feel a strong pull to anything to do with bicycles. If you said, "I love biking but I can't make a living at it," and put this interest on the shelf while tending to the practical challenges of paying the rent, you are doing your purpose a disservice. Choosing to ignore your predisposition for the sake of a larger paycheck elsewhere won't silence this message. Regardless of the path you choose you will always come back to bicycling. It's always going to be a part of you. Further, don't assume that everything is a trade-off. You *can* have it all—just don't confuse the job you do for money with the one you do for life.

You have 8,760 hours each year to spend. If you spend 1,600 hours working and another 2,920 sleeping, this leaves 4,240 hours to spend pampering your predisposition. You could bike halfway around the globe in that time!

Whatever you choose is okay—it's not the choice that matters. Life is not an outcome. It is a game and no matter what you choose, if you've made the big choice to be a winner, you win. If you say, "I really want to spend more time on the golf course, but I can't get away from the pressures at the office," you now have a choice. You

can complain about it or get with the program—
it's okay. It is just the way it is.

The shamans talk about the "wheel of time."
The wheel is made up of many spokes, each lead-
ing in a different direction. Each spoke represents
another path to follow. Unfortunately, we seem
to focus on a single spoke, and, more often than
not, we get stuck. As long as you focus on the
spoke, you are limited and certainty remains elu-
sive. As soon as you focus on the wheel, you bring
unlimited potential into your life. This means
that you now have the ability of 360-degree sight.
You can see in all directions, and that puts you in
a position of certainty. It's how the game of life
needs to be played. Don't begrudge the time you
spend away from those things you feel closest
to—make up for it in other ways.

Acknowledging and honoring your predisposition is the greatest gift you can give yourself. It
opens the doors to unlimited potential.

Wait

Your purpose has a thousand hiding places. It's
like playing hide-and-seek. A really wise child
who has played the game and really wants to win
knows that all he has to do is wait: eventually one
of his friends will giggle or sneeze, revealing her
hiding place.

This strategy is not really about finding your purpose, but setting up the right conditions to let your purpose find you. You can't force the answers—all you can do is ask the questions. You set up the right conditions and know with certainty that if you listen hard enough, you'll hear something.

Early in my career, I was stuck on an accounting problem. I really sweated over it, but as much as I tried, I could not find the answer. Each time I would run the calculations they would show the same mistake. I remember my boss at that time asking me what the problem was. I explained what I had done and that I couldn't find the error. Instead of sitting down with me to help me through to the correct solution, my boss sent me for lunch. I argued that I would rather fix the problem first, then relax at lunch, but he insisted.

"Go for lunch and relax. When you come back, I'm sure you will find the answer," he said.

I remember thinking that this was a really dumb approach. Everything inside me told me to stay, that the answer was obviously quite simple and with more work I was sure to find it. But my boss insisted. He also gave me a copy of the newspaper and said, "While you are at lunch catch up on the news." Now I knew he was crazy. Go for lunch and read the newspaper when I should be hunting for an error? The end of this story is obvious. When I returned from lunch and sat at my desk, lo and behold the answer was right in front of me. It had always been there.

I'm glad I learned this lesson at a young age because there have been hundreds of times when I have been working on problems where the answers eluded me. So, now I take a walk, play my guitar or run on my treadmill to get my mind off the problem. The answer will not necessarily be there the moment I stop, but it will come. Getting away from the problem, busying yourself with something else, is the best solution. Henry David Thoreau wrote, "Success usually comes to those who are too busy to be looking for it."

The same principle applies to those larger questions that lead to your purpose in life. This isn't like trying to complete your taxes or come up with a management solution; these questions are larger in scope and need longer to percolate through your brain. Ask the question then patiently wait for the answer. While you are waiting, get on with life, knowing that eventually an answer will come to you.

Once you have asked the question there is no turning back. Whether you are aware of it or not, your brain is working away at the answer.

Your purpose is not to be a millionaire, politician, doctor or lawyer. Your purpose is to find joy in life. Once you've learned to be more attuned to your predisposition by confronting the unknown and asking the big questions, your unique purpose will become apparent to you, and the joy will follow.

While you're waiting for the answer to appear, however, don't sit back and do nothing. This leads to uncertainty. Incorporate the strategies you are learning in this book into your life. Your positive work will help the answer to percolate more quickly through your brain. When your purpose dawns on you, you'll be ready for the last of our three-part plan, which began with you embracing your significance. This last part of the plan is the most powerful, because it focuses on your intention, which will help you make your purpose a reality.

Creating Certainty from Strategy #5

1. Make a list of all the things you are interested in. This can include such things as golf, gardening, astronomy, watching television, reading, travel, etc.
2. Pretend that someone just told you that your time was limited and you could not do everything on your list. Which items could you eliminate?
3. With the items left on your list, rate each on a scale from one to ten, with ten being very

important and one being something that
would be nice but you could do without.

4. Take the items that ranked highest on your
   list and list activities that incorporate these
   interests into your personal or work life.

5. Ask yourself, "What does this reveal to me
   about my predisposition?"

STRATEGY

6

Think with Clarity

Push away all the noise and
listen to the sounds of the universe.
———— Anonymous ————

Did you know that the human brain can't hold two thoughts at once? It's true! In an article published in the *Toronto Star*, Professor Marcel Just of the Centre for Cognitive Imaging found that our brains cannot do two things well simultaneously. While this knowledge should wake up all those who drive cars while talking on cell phones, the consequences of this study are much farther reaching.

When we focus on one thing at a time our chances of success grow enormously—that's for certain. The trick is knowing where to focus. That's what this strategy is about.

"Multi-tasker" is a label worn by many with pride. The ability to do more than one thing in a society filled with so many opportunities seems an admirable talent. Apparently, multi-tasking is a sought-after skill. There are courses that teach you how to improve your efficiency and if you fail . . . well, you are a failure. To get along in this rush-rush society, we feel the need to do more with the few hours we have each day. We can easily spot the multi-tasking family: four people sit at a table with cells phones, each waiting for the call to action. With one ring, four hands simultaneously reach for the phones.

Multi-tasking is a new phenomenon. Our ancestors had the luxury of focusing all their energy on the task at hand—survival. The cave dwellers measured time by the day, but as society progressed, seconds were divided into tenths, then hundredths, then thousandths and so on. We now measure time in imperceptibly small units. These nanoseconds are relevant in a society where high-speed processing has made available more information than we could possibly use. In a nanosecond, computers can sort, organize and present information to us in as many ways as we can imagine.

We have inflicted upon ourselves a tremendous pressure to mentally measure up with our high-speed processors. We designed these machines to serve humankind, but this master/servant relationship seems to be reversing itself. The human brain and the computer are worlds apart.

I can think back to when I thought it was admirable doing two or three things at a time. It saved time; I could accomplish more in a day. Recently, while driving through the country, I pulled off to the shoulder to watch a farmer prepare his field for seeding. Up and down each row he drove his tractor.

"Wow, I wonder what he is thinking while driving that tractor?" I thought. "What a great opportunity to let the creative juices flow. Maybe he has a tape recorder and . . . hold on, Barry. Maybe he is just driving the tractor rather than driving himself nuts."

Unless we bring multi-tasking into check, we run the real risk of brain clutter. Thinking with clarity involves a process of un-cluttering. It's spring-cleaning for your brain: you throw out what you don't need and leave room for the important stuff.

Recently, I spoke to a self-professed multi-tasker. During our conversation, he admitted that his challenge in life is to eliminate that which he will never do and leave room for those things he will do with certainty. His brain is like a silo filled with wheat, oats and barley. To find the wheat he must sift through the oats and barley—a waste of time and energy.

Overloaded and Unfocused

Lee Iacocca said, "The ability to concentrate and to use your time well is everything." The truth is that multi-tasking creates a noise inside your head that won't go away. It shouts messages from a hundred directions forcing you to pay attention to them all. If you focus on one task, it often leaves you feeling guilty about the others. Guilt of things undone leads to stress, which leads to all sorts of problems: heart disease, neurotic behavior, depression, smoking, addiction—you get the point.

A few months ago, I had dinner with a friend. He talked about his girlfriend, who had just begun a six-month contract to work in Asia. A six-month separation can be difficult for any relationship, so I asked, "Are you going to visit her?"

"I hope so," he answered.

This answer told me the truth. He wasn't going to Asia. If he were, the answer would have been "yes."

This is the same for many of us. We have things we know will be accomplished and those we feel should be accomplished, and the latter items on this list often get left behind.

When you overload your brain with too many tasks, it decreases your chances of successfully completing the things on your mental to-do list and your chances of certainty go out the window. Plato wrote, "Each man is capable of doing one thing well. If he attempts several, he will fail to achieve distinction in any." Certainty, as you have learned, comes from the knowledge that you are doing what you should be doing. If you cloud the picture with lots of irrelevant things, you reduce your chances of a successful conclusion. Your job in this strategy is to do a bit of housecleaning. Take all that brain clutter and organize it, get rid of the irrelevant stuff and focus on what you should be focusing on. To quote a Turkish proverb, "One arrow does not bring down two birds."

Reduce the Noise

With so many chores and thoughts buzzing around in a multi-tasker's head, the important tasks often get lost in the cacophony. We reduce the noise when we eliminate all but the most valuable thoughts in our heads. Easy to say and hard to do. Saying to yourself, "I'm not going to focus on all the unimportant stuff" is like trying not to think about elephants. Yet, as Marcus Aurelius wrote, "A man should remove not only unnecessary acts, but also unnecessary thoughts, for then superfluous activity will not follow."

My editor told me his trick for dealing with mental cacophony. He does all the quick stuff first. So, rather than putting his list in order of importance, he puts it in order of effort. Then with the small tasks out of the way, he can get into the important work with a clear mind. But, what if by the time he cleared up all the small stuff, he couldn't find the time, energy or motivation to focus on important tasks? His solution then is to change venues. He writes in coffee shops. The ambiance of the coffee shop helps him concentrate. Now, we can't all work in coffee shops. Some of us work best alone in the quiet of our bedrooms, others in the office and still others under a tree by a lake. What works for some will not work for others. The trick is finding what works for you.

Like my editor friend, I work best in noisy cafes. I trace this back to my university years when I would study in the student cafeteria. Working in the library put me to sleep. The energy of the people in the cafeteria stimulated me. In my situation, I reduced the noise in my head by increasing the surrounding noise. We all need to find our own way.

There are many tricks that will help us organize our tasks. We could simply list them and call it a day—but this strategy goes much further. You need techniques that you can count on for the long run. It's important to get our internal affairs in order, but how do we determine that order? How do we establish what's really important? This means looking at your tasks in a broader perspective.

Raise the Bar

When we negotiate a business deal or the purchase of a new home, we know our bottom line. We know how low or high we are willing to go in our negotiations. In this principle you are now going to negotiate with yourself. Before you start it is important to set your personal bar high enough to not "give away the farm." Some issues are negotiable and others aren't. Organizing your clutter becomes clearer when you understand the difference between the two.

For many of us it's easier to state what we don't want rather than what we do want. If I asked you where you wanted to be in ten or fifteen years, you might say, "Well, I don't want to have to worry about paying the bills and I don't want to lose my health." Saying what you want is often a more difficult task. The don'ts let you know what where your bottom line is drawn, but the do's are often more positive approaches to achieving your life's purpose.

Once you've reduced your mental noise and asked yourself what you really want, it helps to separate the things that are "nice to have" from the nonnegotiable items–things that no matter what, you are not willing to lose. We have control over nonnegotiables, unlike our money, health or business. At a minute's notice any of these things may be taken from you. You cannot build a life of certainty on sand. The nonnegotiables, however, are rock solid, because, like true significance, they come from you.

Our nonnegotiables help us to determine how we'll deal with ourselves and the world. Instead of settling for our bottom line, working from our nonnegotiables forces us to raise the bar. It means we won't compromise in our actions. How do you want to be remembered? Do you want to die at peace with your world? Do you want to be comfortable with what you have accomplished? Do you want to die alone with your regrets or surrounded by your family and loved ones?

Think about your business. If you had to close the doors tomorrow, how would you want your business remembered? I still hear travelers tell stories about WardAir, an airline in Canada that, while not financially successful, offered a level of customer service that was unparalleled. It set a standard that most other airlines fail even to aspire to. For WardAir, exemplary customer service was nonnegotiable, and as a result, the company is remembered in a way that they wanted.

Nelson Mandela understood this principle. His compassion for his fellow Africans and his understanding of his purpose told him that, no matter what, he was not prepared to negotiate unless the issues most important to him were on the table. Over a period of ten years, the authorities approached Mandela six times with an offer of release—under certain conditions. These conditions were below the bar Mandela had set. He chose prison over freedom because he would not negotiate below his bottom line. When you set your standards on your nonnegotiables, you will give clarity to your life. You'll live the life you want to live, rather than the existence you're prepared to settle for.

Understand Your Intentions

In the last strategy, we looked at our purpose, our big reason for getting out of bed in the morning. Once we've discovered it, our purpose informs everything we do—it forces us to raise the bar. But we can't always be considering such lofty thoughts—like it or not, day-to-day life has to be addressed. We can't abandon our purpose, though—so what should we do?

That's where intention comes in. *Webster's* defines it as "a determination to act a certain way." Purpose is different from intention; purpose suggests a "more settled determination." Imagine that your purpose is the big movie director, envisioning the grand drama. Intention is the movie crew, toiling behind the scenes to make sure that the director's vision comes true. Our intentions help us work toward our purpose. We can imbue our every task with an intention that will allow us to achieve our purpose. Once we unclutter our brain, we can act with clear and strong intentions. Intentions provide us with a structure to use on a daily basis that creates certainty.

I once met a woman who fought a lifelong battle with her weight, which would fluctuate as much as sixty pounds. Her problem was not a lack of motivation or willpower. Her problem was that her intention to lose weight was centered on a specific event. "I want to lose fifteen pounds so I can fit into my new dress for a friend's wedding," she would say and then commence dieting. Many of us focus our intentions on such milestones. It's the "New Year's resolution" mentality.

Sure enough, when the wedding date appeared, she looked great at her desired weight. Within months of the event, however, her weight started to climb and within no time she was back where she had started.

This was not the first time this had occurred, and the repetition of the pattern led to a negative self-image. It was a frustrating experience. In her eyes she was a failure, when she was not a failure at all! She intended to lose weight to attend a wedding and she succeeded. She was a roaring success. It was her intention that was wrong. It was her intention that was limiting.

Another friend of mine had a weight problem and decided that this recurring pattern of gaining and losing weight was like riding a roller coaster and he wanted to get off. He simply no longer wanted to be a fat person. It was affecting his health, he couldn't find clothes that fit and he felt a lack of energy. He was so tired at the end of the day that he was unable to pursue his purpose, which was to be an active and loving husband and father.

"I don't want to be fat anymore. I want to live my life within a healthy weight for my kids and my wife," he stated.

Soon after making this declaration he was entertaining friends at home. One of his friends offered him a plate of chicken wings. He looked at the wings and visualized his fat cells growing. He simply said, "No thanks, chicken wings are inconsistent with my intentions."

His friends were surprised, but my friend had taken the first step toward becoming thinner. From then on, every time he had to make a decision that would impact his health or weight, he would remember his intention to be healthy and fit. Years later, he is still at the weight he wants and is a happy man, able to strive toward his greater purpose.

His intention was to live a life of a thin person. He didn't focus on a specific event, date or time; he began a lifetime journey. With the proper intention, he found the power to live his life of certainty as a thin person.

Imbuing our actions with positive intentions is not as difficult as you may imagine. The spirit is always there inside you, waiting to be put to work. What is needed is the courage to state a life-altering intention, one that is big enough to warrant your attention. Once articulated it takes on a momentum of its own. So how do we work up that courage? This leads us to the next principle.

Pay the Price

Robert was a smoker. He intended to quit his nicotine addiction. The millions who have kicked the habit know how difficult it can be. The price Robert was to pay was nicotine withdrawal. Ex-smokers were encouraging him but he knew he faced a slow, painful and long process. Robert was committed to quitting even though he knew he'd have to pay a price.

So, he began to play games in his mind—games that allowed him to achieve his intention in smaller steps. These bite-size pieces often make the reality of achieving the whole goal possible. Instead of having his morning cigarette he vowed to himself to wait until he reached the office. Once in the office he decided to wait until noon. At noon, he decided to wait until dinner, and after dinner he decided to wait until he walked the dog. Twenty-four hours later he was ready to buy a nicotine patch. Two days later, it still wasn't easy, but now he was ready for a longer commitment, perhaps a whole day or a week. Taking on an intention like this is slow. Eventually, the minutes became hours, which became days, then weeks. Today, thirty years have passed since Robert quit smoking. The games he played helped him cope with his nicotine withdrawal, but they couldn't take it away entirely. Robert knew that to realize his intention, the pain of nicotine withdrawal was a price he'd have to pay.

There is no free lunch. If your intention is worthwhile, it is going to cost you.

In my business, exhibit managers hire me to help their exhibitors. I often conduct seminars. I will also encourage my hosts to place a fee on this seminar for each participant. When we offer this opportunity to exhibitors free, the no-show rate is high. Put a slight value on the experience and the no-show rate drops dramatically. The higher the price the greater the commitment.

The same principle applies to you. Your commitment has a price. It's the cost of living the life you want without the negative behaviors that support an outcome you don't want. It's turning down the next drink or cigarette. It's saying no to the piece of pie or treating your customers or colleagues differently.

I remember once addressing a group of pharmacists. We were in a brainstorming session to develop ways of improving customer service. Many pharmacists stated that their intention was to increase their business with seniors, who could help them to increase their revenue base. We talked about new product lines, moving the pharmacist counter down to eye level, adding an in-store blood pressure monitor and a watercooler so the patient could start his or her medication immediately. Then we spoke about public washrooms. Immediately I heard the cry "We don't want staff spending their day keeping the washroom clean. They have better things to do." The staff agreed that cleaning washrooms was demeaning and not part of the job description. I asked where they thought the seniors ought to go when nature called, and they agreed it was a problem—but they were not willing to budge.

Their intention was to have a friendlier environment for seniors, but the cost of cleaning and stocking a bathroom was more than they were willing to pay. The fact is that if you are not prepared to pay the price—the whole price—there is no point going any further.

The steps to make all your tomorrows better are locked within the daily things you do. You can constantly reinforce the power of certainty by structuring a daily routine that reminds you of what is important. Each small item on your daily agenda becomes a reminder of the journey you are taking. Each act, powered by your intentions, is like making a small deposit into your savings account, building toward a realization of your purpose. Soon the pennies, nickels, dimes and quarters add up to a substantial amount. With each deposit, you reinforce your awareness of your purpose. You now know why you are doing it and where it leads, and the awareness builds. The more you focus on your daily routine the more you will recognize additional opportunities for change. It's like wearing glasses for the first time: suddenly you notice how many other people wear glasses. It's as if we suddenly wake up and see things we missed before. This awareness of purpose, fostered by your intentions, helps maintain your certainty.

Streamlined and Certain

Multi-tasking isn't all that bad, but when we focus our energies, recognize our priorities and really think about the intent behind our actions, committing ourselves to the cost of seeing things through to the end, we are a whole lot more productive and certain. We'll know what we're getting into because we'll have thought things through, rather than running around doing a million things at once, never really managing to work toward our purpose. Thinking with clarity gives us a structure, a strong foundation that allows us to live with certainty.

However, if you read this book and say, "That's very interesting," only to let it gather dust, what's the point? Knowing these six strategies can make a difference, but the last strategy gives them permanence.

Creating Certainty from Strategy #6:

1. Find your place. Not someplace like a tropical island where you'll sip piña colada, but an easily accessible place where your creative juices can flow—a comfortable place where you can reflect without getting caught up in distractions.

2. Once you're settled in your place, make a list of your nonnegotiables. Are there parts of

your life that you would like to change because they are causing you to compromise on
your nonnegotiables? Write down your answers.

3. Decide what small steps you can take immediately to live your life now that you've raised
the bar.

4. In your daily reminder, write down your action steps for tomorrow.

5. Once tomorrow is finished, repeat the exercise for the next day.

STRATEGY

7

Create Lasting Certainty

Great things are not done by impulse,
but by a series of small things brought together.
———— Vincent van Gogh ————

Certainty is like a cell phone battery. It's lifeless without power. A newly charged battery ensures that all channels are sharp and clear, but as the battery loses power so does its efficiency. Left too long and the cell phone is back where it started—unable to fulfill its purpose. We are like the cell phone. Our batteries are charged with excitement when we learn something life altering, like the strategies you have learned in this book. But the excitement fades if not followed by action.

Have you ever come back from a holiday where you spent a couple of weeks unwinding, exploring or lazing in the sun contemplating? You were able to reenter the "real" world with a feeling of euphoria, and all those backed-up phone messages didn't seem quite as important. "If only I could hold on to this feeling," you said to yourself. You know the end of this story: within a few days you were back to your old, pre-vacation self. Where did that suntanning, limbo-dancing, elephant-riding, laughing-out-loud person go? It's so easy to fall back into old habits.

We have all heard of the patient recovering from a near-death experience who vows to change his life. Renewed with a sense of certainty, he swears off old habits and promises to become a more valuable resident of the planet. Sometimes these changes last and other times they are short lived.

Be Your Own Motivator

Friends and colleagues, in trying to label me, ask if I'm a motivational speaker.

"What's that?" I ask.

How can one person motivate someone else? Sure, I can tell a few jokes and get an audience to applaud, but that's not what I am about. If that's all there was, I would look for a different job.

Real motivation to create lasting change requires a plan that lasts beyond the halo effect of reading a book or attending a seminar. No one can make the change for you. No one other than you can ensure that you achieve what you want.

What you need is a structure that will support and maintain your newfound certainty.

Keep Discovering

As you work at integrating certainty into your daily life, the first challenge you face is fighting complacency. Complacency comes when we take routine for granted or let daily actions become habit. In life it's vital to leave as much room as possible for new experiences. If you reach a point where you're satisfied, confident that you've now mastered the game of life, you are selling your potential short. There are always new and exciting aspects of your life to learn about. If you don't keep yourself open to these experiences, you stagnate. It's staying open to these things that helps us make our life stories as complete and rich as possible.

People with multiple interests are better able to cope with brain injuries and diseases than others. By trying new skills and forcing your brain to connect differently, you set up a system where if one part of the brain is injured, another can take over. You'll have taught your brain multiple ways of problem solving. Here we have an opportunity to expand the brain's capacity to maximize your potential for living a life of certainty—but only if we fight complacency.

Not all new experiences work out, but that's not the point. The point is that you won't know until you try.

I used to browse in music stores because I love the look of a guitar. I find it one of the most appealing instruments. So I decided it was my turn and bought an entry-level guitar and a learner's manual. After a few months, I realized that I needed a coach and found someone to give me weekly lessons. I learned the scales and a few chords and, while Eric Clapton has nothing to worry about, I can pluck out a few songs on my guitar.

My guitar has taught me much. I appreciate music more. I understand the genius involved in the creation of music. I can see how people can get lost in their music so that it becomes a form of meditation. I understand how music can bridge cultures and countries, giving people everywhere the same love to share. I better understand the power of rituals based on music.

Has my experience with my guitar helped me? You bet! Think of how much I would have missed if I had never tried. The most amazing thing was that these realizations were all surprises to me. They add to the richness of my life. Try something new and see what surprises are open to you.

New experiences can include anything: music, woodworking, sailing, tennis, golf, bungee-cord jumping, motorcycle racing, learning a language, philosophy, astronomy—anything different from what you do now. Finding the time for these new interests doesn't happen by itself. You have to make room. In Strategy #5 you made a list of all the things you were interested in and ranked them in order of importance. You focused on the top few items to lead you toward your purpose. But what about the rest of the list? There are multitudes of interests open to you. While many of these may not seem earth shattering or particularly important they may just be fun. If you decide that new experiences are a priority in your life, to your amazement, the time will appear and you will wonder why you didn't do it sooner.

I often have people say to me, "Yes, but I have two jobs and three kids and a mother-in-law to take care of. I don't have time for these 'nice-to-haves.'" These individuals are wrapped up in their doubts and fears, but they don't want to free themselves to find something better. My answer is, "Let's play for a moment. Let's suppose that you didn't have two jobs, three children and a mother-in-law. What would you like to do? What activities are you denying yourself?"

They might answer reading—or playing video games. It doesn't really matter. Now that you have identified those "nice-to-haves," the trick is to find the time to do them. I'm amazed by the variety of book titles I see commuters reading when I ride the subway. These busy people find five or ten minutes to read about Zen, yoga or some new skill for "Dummies." There is always time. It's your fears and doubts that hide it. And you'll find that when you take time for these interludes, you'll be able to return to your purpose refreshed and renewed, and with an even stronger sense of certainty.

Take the Time to Take It All In

I once asked a friend what she thought about when she meditated.

"Everything and nothing," she answered. "It's my time to let my soul catch up with my life."

Many of the people I ask have a similar answer. When we're open to everything the universe has to offer, we run the risk of information overload. It is like opening new files on your computer and never taking a moment to save them to your hard drive. You run a real risk of losing important data.

Everyone has their own method of saving the information they've accumulated. You might meditate, play golf, attend religious services or exercise. No one method works for everyone, and there may not be only one method that works for you. Maybe you can do several things to save this information. In the last strategy you learned the importance of finding "your place." Whether it is a noisy coffee shop, a busy airport waiting area or your place of worship, find that place and start saving the valuable information that you've taken in.

When I play my guitar, I am lost in the music. For twenty or thirty minutes I think of nothing else. When I sing along with my guitar strumming, a powerful connection is made. It no longer matters how I sound. I am with the music. Whether you are taking a hike in a forest or sailing over blue waters, finding the time to absorb new experiences is important. Don't let anything slip out of your grasp—because, as we know, each experience is significant.

Lasting Certainty

One of my earliest memories is of my grandparents' home. Nailed to the back of the storage-room doors were small tin cans. Each can—*pishka*—was labeled for a different charity. These *pishkas* were reminders that other people need our help, so our ritual was to drop our pennies or nickels in these boxes. Today, when I shop with my daughter and watch her drop coins into the *pishkas* on the counter tops of convenience stores, memories of my grandparents' home come flooding back.

Stephen, who is a busy manager, always walks around the city with quarters in his pockets. When a homeless or destitute person asks for help, Stephen always responds. I once asked him why and his answer was simply, "Because I can."

I live in rural Ontario. Our small town is home to a family who, every Christmas, give us all a present. For months they plan, organize and build their Christmas-light show. Their home becomes a luminescent wonderland filled with moving characters and wonderful messages. They invite everyone to walk their property and enjoy the sight. People come from miles away to see this annual display of giving. This family's only motivation is to give something back to their town.

A lifetime of giving is probably the easiest reminder of the principles of significance, purpose and intentions. Remember the rabbi's conversation I told you about in Strategy #4. You don't have to give money; you could donate some of your time to read to a child, or you could organize an outing, feed the hungry, build homes for the homeless, help the elderly carry parcels, let another motorist enter your lane—the list is endless. But with each act, the trick is to tell yourself, "It's because that's the kind of person I am."

Looking Back and Moving Forward

So, that's it—almost.

You have learned that there is a natural cycle to everything. Nothing is stagnant. If it's not working out for you now—it will. You also know that you have a choice as to how you want to live—choose to live like a winner. You know that the roadblocks in your path are really just doubts in disguise, and you know how to face them proactively. You have learned a more meaningful way to understand your significance and purpose, and you're able to think clearly. And now, you know that if you stay motivated and keep exploring throughout your journey, incorporating the knowledge you gather into your life, you will create lasting certainty. The only thing left is to do the work.

Creating Certainty from Strategy #7

1. Revisit the list of things you are interested in that you created in Strategy #5.
2. The items on the top of the list helped guide you to your predisposition and purpose, but now it's time to deal with the rest of the list. Write a plan for incorporating some of these items into your daily life immediately.
3. What other changes can you make that will reinforce what you have learned in this book?

What's Next?

Now you have read and worked through the seven strategies to certainty. Don't assume your job is complete. It's not. It has only begun. You have to do the work. Certainty is not a matter of wishing it so. It involves much hard work.

Have you heard the joke about a man who went to church to pray?

"God," he said, "if you will only let me win the lottery everything will be fine. It's not for me, God, it's for my family. My wife needs extensive medical care and it's going to be expensive, and my daughter is going to college and I can't afford her tuition. I have always been a righteous man and this is the first time I have really asked for something. Please grant me this one wish."

Then he went home and waited. When they announced the lottery winners, his name was not on the list. So, the next week he went back to church and prayed again.

"Maybe you didn't understand," he began. "I have always been a righteous man and this prayer is not for me, it is for my wife and daughter. If you will only let me win the lottery, I can give them the help they deserve."

Again he went home and after the next draw searched vainly for his name amongst the lottery winners. Nothing. So, once more he prayed.

"Dear God. I really need your help. The lottery winnings are crucial for me to take care of my wife and daughter. I have always been a good man and never asked for things for myself. This is the third time I've asked and I'm not sure you are listening. Why won't you help me?"

Just then a bright light appeared before his eyes and he heard the voice of God saying, "Work with me, Saul. Buy a ticket."

This hard work is like paying your dues. Everyone has to do it. You can't win the lottery without buying a ticket. Before an actor gets to work in a movie or onstage, she must first learn his craft, then go through the laborious task of auditions. Day after day, week after week, more auditions and more rejections. Then lightning strikes and a bit part is thrown her way. She does the part and goes back to the drudgery of auditions. During this process, she may take roles for no pay or she may end up waiting tables in a local deli.

You can't walk into a movie studio and expect to be a star, and you can't barge into the boardrooms of General Motors or Microsoft and expect to become the next president without some experience behind you. You have to develop enough experience to know that you can handle the job.

This process of paying dues has little rewards along the way. We get glimpses of success. Bit parts, small writing assignments or the closing of a small deal. When they happen, don't dismiss them as luck or coincidence—you know better. Moviemaker Samuel Goldwyn once said, "The harder I work, the luckier I get." These small accomplishments are the universe's way of saying, "It's okay, you are on the right track."

These seven strategies require daily diligence. They require accepting rejection and understanding how the game of life is played. You must pay your dues, but if you work with determination, nothing can stop you from attaining certainty. Then—and only then—will you soar with the eagles.

Epilogue

I have a friend named Gail with whom I hadn't spoken in many years. She and her partner, Dan, used to live in Toronto, and my wife and I used to get together with them at least twice a month. We would eat, laugh and enjoy each other's company. Gail's energy was always the highlight of an evening. Her quirky storytelling and her infectious laughter helped set the tone for any dinner party.

About ten years ago Dan's job took him and Gail out to Vancouver's suburbs. Gail wasn't thrilled with the idea of leaving Toronto but she loved Dan, so she made the move with him. Gail and I would talk occasionally on the phone, and a couple of times we made the effort to travel and visit each other, but as the years passed, the time between phone calls grew greater, and the visits just stopped happening.

Last winter, out of the blue, Gail called me. She had seen an article in the paper about my upcoming seminar in Vancouver all about *Eagles Must Soar*. She told me that she was planning on attending, and invited me to have lunch with her after it was done. I couldn't put my finger on exactly what it was at the time, but her voice on the phone sounded a little lost. But I didn't think much more about it until I saw her in Vancouver a month later.

She sat through my seminar, laughed at all my jokes, dutifully took notes and seemed to be quite intrigued by what I was saying, but still I could tell that something was not quite right. The sparkling Gail I had known for so many years seemed missing. Afterwards, when we went for lunch, I found out why.

She began by telling me that she and Dan had split up earlier that year. Things hadn't been good in quite a while and last year they had finally and painfully decided to part ways. Since then Gail's life had been an emotional roller-coaster ride. Her job contract had ended, and her only child, Jessica, had gone off to university. Suddenly she was left with a whole lot of time on her hands, most of which she spent thinking about her life.

"There were times in your seminar this morning when I felt like you were talking right to me," she began. "For the last few years, I have felt lost, like I have forgotten about who I really am. My path has seemed hazy to me. I feel like I haven't been certain about anything in a long, long time."

"You're not alone in that one," I replied. "When we get wrapped up in the details of life it can be really easy to forget our real predisposition. That's common. But that's why it's not a bad idea to have a little help from time to time to remind us how we can make choices with certainty and clarity. Everyone needs that."

"I know," she said, "I know. I think you wrapped it up for me in Strategy #3, when you talked about fear being a reaction to something very real, and doubt being a response to what we are afraid of. Over the last year I've felt held hostage by fear—fear because my job ended, and I'm afraid that I might not ever find work again. Fear because my marriage split up, and I'm afraid that I won't ever find love again. And fear that, with my daughter moving off to university, I'm no longer needed as a mother."

"Those are all scary things," I told her. "But I'll bet if you look into all of those in more detail, you may find that some of the stuff contributing to those thoughts are more doubts than fears. Nevertheless, it all seems very real to you, and all of it must be dealt with."

"I know," she said, "and one of the things that hit home this morning was when you talked about harnessing the power of our fears. You said they make us who we are. That is so true. My fears are my own, and I have no doubt that there are loads of wonderful information in them that can help me live my life. Right now it's tough to separate myself from the fears in order to be able to see that clearly. But I can't tell you how empowering that was for me to hear you say that."

"It's true," I said. "Fears make us who we are. It's knowing how to harness their power, as opposed to letting them become obstacles, that's the trick. It's recognizing that these fears are actually there to smooth out the road for you, not just block it. And I know that it's hard. I struggle with it all the time. But recognize that you've taken a pretty huge step in a positive direction."

She continued, telling me about how she sometimes feels that her head is running off in all kinds of different directions. "I'd like to travel to South America," she began, "and I'd like to start my own consulting company, and I'd like to go back to school and learn another language, and I'd like to bake my own bread...but I know that

I'm not going to accomplish all that. Most of the stuff on my to-do list has been there for twenty years! Hearing you talk about finding the things on my list that I am actually committed to and discarding all the rest suddenly makes my life seem a whole lot easier. I'm never going to bake my own bread. And I know that because I've never so much as opened a cookbook to find out how. That's one that I can disregard easily!"

I responded, "I'll bet if you make the list I talked about in the sixth strategy you may find there are even more things on there you can cross off. I did it myself years ago. It changed my life. Having only a few goals that all related to my real predisposition, rather than having a great many that I would never accomplish, left me with a real sense of focus. Subconsciously I never truly intended to accomplish them anyway. It became such a liberating process for me. I felt a clarity that I hadn't felt in years."

Her eyes began to light up as she spoke. "I know. For years I followed my backup plan. I wanted to start my own consulting company, but instead I spent years gathering qualifications that would allow me to work in an institution. I chose what I thought would be a safer path, one that I felt would allow me to be a good wife and mother, but that path didn't allow me to be a whole person. And I'm not saying that being a good wife and mom weren't part of my path, because they are and were a wonderful part of it. But years ago I stopped having the confidence to listen to myself. I stopped having certainty about who I was. And I started making compromises in my life that didn't reflect my passion."

"I know exactly what you're talking about," I told her in response. "And, as we talked about in the seminar, living with certainty may not be any less bumpy a journey, but you probably won't feel the bumps quite as much because your soul will know that the trip is worthwhile—whatever the cost."

"And it all has a natural flow!" she said, getting more animated than I had seen her all morning. "I really needed to hear that. I now know that this low I'm currently in will turn around. That I'll be soaring once again. Thank you for reminding me."

"It's my pleasure," I told her. "You probably already knew everything I told you in the seminar this morning. It's just that sometimes we need a little reminding."

"That's the understatement of the year!" she said, emitting that infectious laugh I hadn't heard in many, many years. "I bought a couple of copies of your book this morning. One for me and one for my daughter. I have no doubt that she can use this as well. If only someone had given me your book when I was her age—or for that matter any age!" She laughed again. This was the Gail that I used to know.

We paid the bill, left the restaurant and promised to keep in touch. I have no doubt that Gail will discover how to live her life with certainty. I have no doubt that, with a little help, we all can.

Index

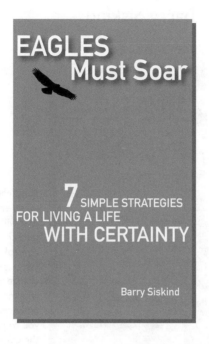

Also by Barry Siskind

Bumblebees Can't Fly offers seven easy-to-learn strategies that will give you the power to take charge of your life and control your own destiny. In a fast-paced world of rapid change and sometimes overwhelming options, it is a practical guide that will help you to stay productive using the common sense you already have. If you follow the seven simple strategies in Bumblebees Can't Fly, you, too, will find your pot of honey at the end of the day.

From John Wiley & Sons Canada, Ltd.
ISBN: 0-470-83439-0